Fight Back
Principles of War

Tool Box Kit

FIGHT BACK
WEAPONS OF WARFARE

COGNITIVE BEHAVIORAL MODELS FROM A BIBLICAL PERSPECTIVE

Dr. Stacy D. Coward, RN, LPC, ThD

Tree House Ministries Publishing

Tree House Ministries Publishing Products are available at special quantity for bulk purchases for the sales and promotions premium fundraiser and educational needs. For details write to 3615 Victory Blvd Portsmouth, Virginia 23704 or email stacy.coward@yahoo.com

UOM, Inc Tree House Ministry Products are available at special quantity for bulk purchases for the sales and promotions premium fundraiser and educational needs.

Fight Back
Principles of War

For more details write: 3615 Victory Blvd, Ste 105
Portsmouth, Virginia 23704, stacy.coward@yahoo.com
(757) 581-3897, Face book, UOM, Inc Counseling

Design by the UOM, Inc Tree House Ministry Products:
ISBN 978-1-300-51442-8
Imprint: Lulu.com

Fight Back
Principles of War

I write this book to share principles about how to fight back. The devil is tricky he knows how to beat you up to a place where you feel homicidal or suicidal. If you're not careful he'll catch you when your guard is down spiritually, emotionally and physically beat you down. This book is written to help you learn how to put your dukes up and fight back.

It doesn't have anything to do with a physical fight because the word of God plainly teaches us it is not by power not by might but by his spirit that we prevail.

There so many times when I am under attack that my flesh really wants to respond. I have learned I lose every time when my flesh responds. I have to respond in the spirit realm.

Fight Back
Principles of War

I want to teach you some principles or responding and fighting the spirit realm and harnessing your flesh. This book is written to be a guide in appropriate fighting. It is both practical and biblical based. As a goal to provide the readers with the tools they need to be successful in beating challenging circumstances.

If you are going to win you have to learn how to fight the good fight. You have to learn how to fight in a way that does not damage the people you love nor yourself. As a teenage mother I had a lot of struggles. I became a fighter early because I realized that if I was going to make it I had to fight. The problem was that I was fighting everybody including the people I loved. It wasn't until years later that I learned what productive fighting looked like. I had to learn how to fight the war in the spirit and in the natural. I had to learn how to take all of my energy and harness it then focus it on the right

Fight Back
Principles of War

people, places and things. Now, I will say that this is not been an easy task but I want to use the information I have learned along the way to make your journey easier. It is a continual growing process. I must continue to work on being productive in my warring techniques.

Preparing For Battle

Get your mind right! You must know without a shadow of a doubt that you are in a war and there really is a battlefield. Each battlefield requires a new set of weapons. An important key is to know which tools you need for each battlefield. You are always at war! Never believe that you can afford to go on spiritual sabbatical, vacation or hiatus. You are never out of the danger zone. You are either in the battle, coming out of the battle or preparing for the battle. Make no mistake in your understanding there is a war. The sooner you recognize that you must be on guard and prepared for the battle the position you will be in when you come under attack.

PART ONE

WHAT IS THE FIGHT ABOUT

We asked those questions because you must know what you are fighting for?

How can you fight a good fight when you do not know what you are fighting for?

This section is designed to help you evaluate what your fight is about? It will help you to narrow down what is most important for you and why you are doing what you are doing

Let's learn how to fight the right way!

Knowing who you are is half the battle. You are fearfully and wonderfully made let us see what makes you tick as you start your journey towards your wonderful life.

Who am I and where am I going?

1 year from right now

_____

_____

_____

_____

5 years from right now

_____

_____

_____

Fight Back
Principles of War

_____

_____

10 years from right now

_____

_____

_____

_____

_____

_____

_____

When it's all said and done what will be the
story they say about who I was as a person

_____

_____

_____

_____

_____

_____

Fight Back
Principles of War

Take a good look at yourself

1. What makes you laugh?
2. What makes you feel most authentic?
3. What makes you think about your life?
4. What makes you concerned?
5. What happens when you become afraid?
6. What do your best days look like?
7. What do your worst days look like?
8. When are you tired?
9. When do you know you have you given your all?
10. What do you procrastinate on?
11. What motivates you to action?
12. What makes you stumble when you are doing well?
13. How many people do you need around you to do well?
14. What does a good team look like for your like?
15. What do you like most about yourself?
16. What do you want to change about yourself?

Fight Back
Principles of War

17. What do you feel most passionate about?
18. What makes you angry?
19. What makes you cry?
20. When are you happiest?
21. Who is around you when you are happiest?
22. What are you doing when you are most happy?
23. What makes you anxious?
24. What ideas excite you most?
25. When do you do the best?
26. How much money is enough?
27. What makes your life feel quality?
28. Where do you want to visit?
29. What do you want to change about yourself
30. What do you want to improve about your appearance?

Fight Back
Principles of War
From the List

What words are repeating?

What ideas keep appearing?

What is the connection or theme you hear in
your words

If the word, phrase or idea has appeared 3 or
more times its important for you.

Self-awareness is the first key to fighting
because you have to know what it is that you're
fighting and why.

Fight Back
Principles of War
DREAM HOUSE

If you had the ability to create whatever life you wanted tell me the life you would imagine for yourself

_____
_____
_____
_____
_____
_____
_____
_____
_____
_____

Evaluate yourself before anyone else has to evaluate your life. You are able to look at your life and know when enough is enough. Do not wait for someone else to tell you about your life.

Fight Back
Principles of War

Circle **YES or NO**

Do you have enough rest time?   **YES or NO**

Do you have the furniture you want in your home? **YES or NO**

Do you have enough family time? **YES or NO**

Are you exercising?   **YES or NO**

Are you generally healthy? **YES or NO**

Can you purchase any food you would like to eat? **YES or NO**

Do you have a saving account with three months of income? **YES or NO**

Do you have good credit? **YES or NO**

Can you go to on vacation with planning? **YES or NO**

Can you purchase anything you want at anytime for under $ 500 **YES or NO**

Fight Back

Principles of War

Are you living in your dream home? **YES or NO**

Are you living your best life? **YES or NO**

Do you have enough resources to do what you think is important? **YES or NO**

Do you have money left after you pay your bills? **YES or NO**

Do you like the car you are driving? **YES or NO**

Do you have friends that can help you? **YES or NO**

Do you have a pet? **YES or NO**

Do you spend enough quality time with your family? **YES or NO**

You Get To Choose

You choose your life and how you live your life. The key is to know that you always have a choice for your life and you get to decide what your life looks like. Choose to make your life the way you envision it and it does not have to come from a place of tragedy. It can come as a result of you making a conscious decision about what you choose. As you are deciding what you are going to put your energy into, review the list that you completed so you have a clear picture of who you are.

Fight Back
Principles of War

Draw a picture of the life you would like to have

Fight Back
Principles of War
Point it where it hurts

As a nurse patient would often come in and say I am hurting and I would say can you tell me where? They would generally use their hand and say right in hear. Then I would say, "Use one finger and point to it. Point to exactly where it hurts. Sometimes they could and sometimes they could not. In other words sometimes the pain was so extensive it just hurt everywhere. We had to deal with all the places that they were having pain before we could narrow down where the problem was. Then there were other times when we caught it early enough where they could point to the one place they were hurting. Either way we had to identify the place of pain so we could know what we needed to fix.

Fight Back
Principles of War

What areas in your life do you need to be honest with yourself about so you can improve?

Where does it hurt?

_____

_____

_____

_____

_____

_____

_____

_____

_____

_____

_____

_____

_____

_____

_____

_____

Fight Back
Principles of War

Use the list below to help you put your thoughts into words

Point to it

- o My bills take all my money
- o My relationship with my spouse
- o My children don't appreciate my efforts
- o My lack of education
- o I regret my mistakes
- o I don't feel productive
- o I am not growing in my church
- o My in laws are not supportive
- o I had a rough childhood
- o My relationship with my friend
- o My best friend hurt me
- o I feel betrayed by my spouse
- o I am being taken advantage of
- o Feeling taken for granted
- o I was cheated on
- o I was mistreated by a person
- o My job does not respect me
- o I don't have enough free time
- o I don't like myself
- o I am not happy on my job

Fight Back
Principles of War

What do you need to change about
yourself that is causing you to have
difficulty in your everyday life?

What paradigms (The way you view the
world from your perspective) has to be
shifted in order for you to grow?

Tender Spots

They make you vulnerable during the battle

Let's deal with the places in your life that are stopping you from being the best version of yourself. Deal with your own issues first. Take your eyes off of everyone else and place them on yourself. Look at yourself and take full responsibility for your life at this moment. Hold yourself accountable for your life and your actions

YOU ARE NOW RESPONSIBLE FOR YOUR CHANGE

What are your weaknesses?

What does your family and close friends tell you that you keep doing wrong?

What does your supervisor say your weakness is?

What do you think you can improve to be a more quality person or employee?

What do you lack that is keeping you from getting what you want?

How are you wasting your time?

Principal Fighting Keys

Fearless Fighting

You must learn it you cannot be afraid
and be in the fight. They can smell your
fear on you when you are fighting. Most
of the time, you have to fight like you are
crazy. The tenacity in which you are
fighting from does not come unless you
fight like your life depends on it. You
have to make up in your mind that you
ain't scared of nothing. This level of
fighting is not even about your bark. It
truly is about your bite. You might hit me
but I'm still going to bite you in the
middle of this fight. If you fool around and
let me get up you surely better kill me
because I'm not going to stop until you
do! I'm not afraid of the sting of death in
this fight. After I get hit if you let me get
up I'm coming after you. Fighting like this

Fight Back
Principles of War

is a completely different level of fighting.
When you are fighting from this place
there is no such animal as quit, I'm hurt, I
can't, I need. All I need is the will to keep
going and even if I got to creep, crawl, roll
or slide, I am getting to where I am I
trying to go.

We have to learn how to war in the spirit
as though your life depended on it.
Ultimately, it really does. You may think
it's all fun and games, laughs and jokes,
heroes and zeros, but the reality of it is
that you are in a fight and cannot be afraid.
Fight with no fear and refuse to die!

Fight Back
Principles of War

We are all human. Sometimes the enemy does look scary. When you become afraid proclaim the word *that God has not given me a spirit of fear but of power love and sound mind!*

I shall live and not die to proclaim the word of the Lord!

Knowing What to Fight for

You're in the wrong fight. It's not even your business. Nobody cares what your opinion is. They don't need your money, your time or your energy. They really can figure it out by themselves.

Why are you over there arguing about their lives and their situation? Ultimately, everyone must learn on their own sweat and blood. It is not your job to save the world especially your adult children. Stop getting involved in fights that are not yours to battle.

Fight Back
Principles of War

Identify the 5 W's

Identify the demographic of people WHO you are attempting to fight for?

Who are you fighting for?

_____

What do they look like? _____

How old are they? _____

Where do they live? _____

How many people? _____

Identify exactly WHAT you are trying to accomplish with or for this group you are fighting for.

What are your fighting for?

Pinpoint the ideas that you are trying to establish

What is the mission?

_____

Fight Back
Principles of War
What do you envision for this group?

_____

Identify the timeline WHEN you will work?

When are you fighting for this cause?

When does it start? _____When
does it stop?_____

How many days during the week will you work
on this project or program?_____

How will you gage when it is finished?

_____

Identify the expertise WHERE you will fight

Where are you going to fight?

What area of expertise will you maximize
in and become the subject matter expert in.
In order to become the most effective in
the area identify your area and capitalize
on it.

Biggest Question: WHY is this important for you and how will you translate the importance of this fight to the people you are trying to help?

Why are you fighting this particular fight?

_____

_____

_____

_____

_____

Your why will be the energy needed to fuel your activities when you find yourself running out of fight stamina. It will be the focal place for you to get redirected and encouragement to continue the fight even when opposition comes.

Fight Back
Principles of War

Do they know you are fighting for them?

_____

Do they want your
help?_____

Are they ready for your
help?_____

Are you equipped to fight for
them?_____

What are some resources you will need to be the
most effective?

_____

Is this fight for you or is it for them?

_____

How do you know what you are doing is
meaningful?_____

Fight Back
Principles of War

What are your measurable outcome?

_____

How many people did you fight for during this
particular time?_____

Fight Back
Principles of War
Fight to Finish

Sweep the trash up out of the middle of
the floor. We must learn how to fight to
finish everything we started. Something as
simple as not sweeping the trash up and
putting it in the trashcan indicates that you
will not finish things. If you will sweep
up the trash but leave it in the middle of
the floor then you certainly will not finish
the more important things. When you're
tired you want to give up that is the time to
fight get to the finish. Tomorrow is not
promised you may not get a chance to
finish. You have an opportunity to finish
something always choose to finish it even
if you don't use it you finished it.

Knowing When Fight Is Over

Why do you keep picking up something and fighting for and left a long time ago. You have to quickly learn how to look at your situation and see where you are today sometimes where you were 10 years ago is no longer the place where God would have you to be now.

You must evaluate your life and no you are in the right place at the right time and the right season. God is assigned us Ecclesiastics 3: 10 with the time, a purpose and a season during a particular time. No use in trying to live in a season that is long gone. You must know when the fight is over so you can move on to the next fight.

Stop Picking Fights with Yourself that don't count

You don't have to fight against yourself. Too many times people pick fights with themselves that do not count. Are you fighting with situations, people or ideas that have moved on from you? My niece Robin once said, "Auntie, I had to learn how to stop fighting myself on things that were only hurting me. I picked up an idea some years ago and because I chose it. I refused to put it down even though I knew it was no longer valid. I kept fighting to keep it alive but I was only hurting me." It was profound. The fact that she recognize that she was fighting herself on some ideas that nobody even cared about. She didn't even care about it but because she had said she wasn't going to do it she continued to

Fight Back
Principles of War

fight not to give up the idea. She said I woke up one day and said, "I decided it was okay for me to change my mind." I don't have to fight with myself anymore to prove to myself that I can do something that my heart is no longer in. I'm not fighting with me anymore.

Take Action

Name three weak areas you would like to
work on to improve yourself

90 Days	1 Year	5 Years
1. 2. 3.	1. 2. 3.	1. 2. 3.

Accountability

How will you hold yourself accountable for
making the changes?

Who will you tell to look behind you to make
sure you are doing what you said you were
going to do?

Timeline

Fight Back
Principles of War

How much time is reasonable to make the changes?

What is a reasonable pace for you to work?

How often will you work on your goal of improve

What time of day works best for you?

How can you make the changes without stressing yourself out?

Measurable

How will you know when you are finished?

How will you know that you are making progress?

Two Dates with a Dash in the Middle- NOT!!

Where will you leave your mark in the world?

Who will your family say that you were as a caregiver?

How will the community remember your life's work?

New

Weapons

Fight Back
Principles of War

Use your Mouth

Only pray the Word of God .Don't waste your voice power of empty words. Pray the scriptures and the scriptures alone. Look up scriptures for the area you have concern in and individualize the scripture and pray the scripture. Remember the Holy Spirit responds to His word. Here are a few examples that you can use to format effective prayer language that penetrates the spirit realm.

Create
YOUR PRAYER LIST

_____

_____

_____

_____

_____

_____

_____

_____

Fight Back
Principles of War

I declare and I decree the Word of God

Is. 54:17 *No weapon that is formed against me
will prosper; and every tongue that accuses me
in judgment my God will condemn. God your
word declare that this is my heritage because I
am servant of the Lord, and their vindication is
from you Lord*

*I am self-controlled and I am alert. Even
though my enemy the devil prowls around like a
roaring lion looking for someone to devour. I
resist him and I stand firm in the faith according
to **1 Pet. 5:8-9***

*Yes Lord, you are faithful, and You Lord will
strengthen me and protect me from the evil one
as I stand in your promises from **2 Thess. 3:3***

*Lord I stand on your word and I know that I
conquer the enemy by the blood of the Lamb and*

Fight Back
Principles of War

*by the word of my testimony, **Rev.12:11** And my testimony is that I am more than a conqueror.*

Lord I believe that whatever I bind on earth will be bound in heaven, and whatever I loose on earth will be loosed in heaven. Therefore I bind every demonic attack upon my life and the people who I love. I bind anything that would hinder my progress. I bind the spirits that are assigned to be a distraction to me. I loose every stronghold, every generational curse, every spiritual legal contract that I have made or my ancestors have made over me and my children's children. I loose every legal obligation that has been set in motion as a result of my ancestors contracts, sins and penalties.

*I stand in full agreement with your Word and I believe that if two of you on earth agree about anything they ask for, it will be done for them by my Father in heaven." **Matt. 18:18-19** Therefore Lord we ask believing you for the changes in our family, work, community, relationships, finances, health and wisdom.*

Fight Back
Principles of War

Use your voice tone

Shout to God with a voice of triumph and songs of joy! Psalms 47:2

Use your hands

Psalms 18:34 He trains my hands for battle; my arms can bend a bow of bronze
Psalms 47:1 - O clap your hands, all ye people; shout unto God with the voice of triumph.
Psalms 98:8 - Let the floods clap their hands: let the hills be joyful together

Isaiah 55:12 - For ye shall go out with joy, and be led forth with peace: the mountains and the hills shall break forth before you into singing, and all the trees of the field shall clap their hands.

Ezekiel 25:6 - For thus saith the Lord GOD;

Fight Back
Principles of War

Because thou hast clapped thine hands, and stamped with the feet, and rejoiced in heart with all thy despite against the land of Israel;

Job 27:23 - Men shall clap their hands at him, and shall hiss him out of his place.

2 Kings 11:12 - And he brought forth the king's son, and put the crown upon him, and gave him the testimony; and they made him king, and anointed him; and they clapped their hands, and said, God save the king.

Nahum 3:19 - There is no healing of thy bruise; thy wound is grievous: all that hear the bruit of thee shall clap the hands over thee: for upon whom hath not thy wickedness passed continually?

Lamentations 2:15 - All that pass by clap their hands at thee; they hiss and wag their head at the daughter of Jerusalem, [saying, Is] this the city that men call The perfection of beauty, The joy of the whole earth?

Fight Back
Principles of War

Use Your Angels

Rank Structure

King James Bible Eph 6:12

For we wrestle not against flesh and blood, but against principalities, against powers, against the rulers of the darkness of this world, against spiritual wickedness in high *places*.

1st Sphere – Seraphim, Cherubim and Thrones

2nd Sphere – Dominions, Virtues and Powers

3rd Sphere – Principalities, Archangels and Angels.

SERAPHIM – sometimes called "the burning ones" because they are closest to God and radiate Pure Light. These are the Angels who constantly sing God's praise, and whose duty it is to regulate the heavens. (Lucifer is said to

Fight Back
Principles of War

have been one of the Seraphim who had outshone all the others until

he became the head of the fallen angels).

CHERUBIM – sent to guard the gates of Eden. Originally they were depicted as the bearers of God's Throne, as the charioteers, and as powerful beings with four wings and four faces. However, in modern times, Cherubim have evolved into chubby babies with wings.

THRONES – called the 'many eyed ones' have the duty of carrying out God's decisions. They are often represented as firey wheels.

DOMINIONS – their job is to regulate the duties of the other Angels and ensure that God's wishes are carried out.

VIRTUES – the Angels of Grace who bring God's blessings to Earth, usually in the form of miracles. Known as the 'brilliant' or "shinning'" ones, they are associated with acts of heroism and bring courage when needed.

Fight Back
Principles of War

POWERS – their job is to prevent the 'fallen angels' from taking over the world and keeping the Universe in balance. They are also seen as the Angels of birth and death.

PRINCIPALITIES – the Guardian Angels of cities, nations and rulers, and guards against the invasion of evil angels.

ARCHANGELS – probably the best known of all Angels. They carry God's most important messages to humans. They also command God's 'armies' of Angels in the constant battle with the "sons of darkness."

ANGELS – the Celestial Beings closest to humans. They act as intermediaries between the Almighty and humanity. Often called our "Guardian Angels."

Angels only respond to God's Word and are sent to carry out His will in our lives.

Fight Back
Principles of War

> *""Bless the Lord, you His angels, who are mighty, and do His commands, and obey the voice of His word. Bless the Lord, all you His hosts; you servants who do His pleasure." (**Psalm 103:20-21**, MEV)*

And God said in Isaiah 55:11 that His Word will not return to Him void. In other words, when the Word of God is spoken out of the mouth of a believer, it is the same as God the Father speaking it, and the angels hearken unto God's Word spoken by a believer the same way they do when God himself gives a command from His throne!

Fight Back
Principles of War

When we return the Lord's Word to Him, angels
are supernaturally dispatched to carry out the
fulfillment of the Scripture and Word of God.
Other translations of this Scripture declare that
angels both listen for His Word and are
responsible for executing Scripture according to
the way He intends the Word to be fulfilled. If
we want our prayers and declarations to be
successful, it is vitally important to utilize the
Word of God

Fight Back
Principles of War
Fight to show love

Sometimes you do not feel like being
lovely and kind and pure and gentle and
meek and humble and self-controlled. I
understand. Those are the times when you
must dig deep to fight to show love. We
must learn how to show the fruit of the
spirit even when it does not feel good.
Showing love can be hard to do especially
when you're not getting the love back
keep showing it I watch God for miracle in
your life.

Fight to Maintain Integrity

Always do the right thing even when nobody is watching. Your integrity will keep you safe. It is a fight sometimes to do the right thing especially when everybody else is doing the wrong thing. Your job is to fight the urge to do it wrong. On the days that you feel weak you are playing the game towards cheating fight the urge and do what is right.

Fight to Be an Example

You must maintain a sense of responsibility the right thing. You are an example someone. Somebody is watching what you're doing fight to be a good example. When in doubt think about the person who is learning how to live, love, work and even play by watching you. You are somebody's role model be a great example.

Fight for Your Life

What do you envision your life to become you must be the first responder fire fighter for your life. Nobody is giving you anything and is going to be hot many days. You must learn how to quickly assess the environment and put the fires out immediately. Must day in a state of the first responder for your life. No one should have to tell you that you're doing too much. No one should have to tell you that your life is out of hand. Your job is to look at your life evaluated for hot situations and extinguishes the fires.

Fighting in the Flesh

If the conversation ended up in a cussing
match you were in the flesh. You may
have very well meant well however
somewhere along the line you were
offended hurt or frustrated so you started
fighting with the flesh. As soon as you
recognize that you are in the flesh end the
conversation. There is a better way to get
your feelings heard by the other party. The
trouble with fighting the flesh is that
someone always gets hurt. You end up
with holes in the wall, holes in hearts,
holes in relationship, holes everywhere.
Fighting in the flesh always produces
holes.

Now GO and **FIGHT A GOOD FIGHT!**

Fight Back
Principles of War